my Lily

Donal created this book a few months before
he was diagnosed with Stage 4 Neuroblastoma,
a very rare children's cancer.

Donal is currently completing 18 months
of aggressive treatment at
Our Lady's Children's Hospital, Crumlin, Dublin.

Donal loves his dog and she has helped
him cope with this extremely difficult time.

My dog is called Nelly

She is scared of balloons

My dog likes to go for runs

She can
not play fetch

My dog likes to lie on the sofa

She runs away from bicycles

My dog steals my Dad's lunch

And she likes eating my lego

I love my dog

Donol wrote
this book
and he
drew pictures

WHAT IS NEUROBLASTOMA?

Neuroblastoma is a rare cancer which affects an average of 10 children a year in Ireland. It often occurs in young children under the age of 5. It is a cancer of specialised nerve cells called neural crest cells. These cells are involved in the development of the nervous system and other tissues.

Neuroblastoma often begins in the abdomen. The two main areas it can affect are the adrenal glands and the nerve tissue at the back of the abdomen. It can spread to other parts of the body, such as the bone marrow, bones, liver and skin, through the blood and lymph nodes.

Donal was diagnosed with stage 4 Neuroblastoma with MYCN amplification, a more aggressive type of the disease. The cancer had spread from his abdomen to his eyes, bones and lungs. As with most cancers, the cause of Neuroblastoma is not known.

One of the features of Neuroblastoma is the high rate of relapse. In the event of a relapse Donal's options for treatments that can cure the disease may be limited to clinical trials and new treatments that are only available outside Ireland.